MUSIC FROM THE MOTION PICTURE SOUNDTRACK
ARRANGED FOR PIANO
DARKEST HOUR

MUSIC BY DARIO MARIANELLI

ISBN: 978-1-5400-3414-4

HAL•LEONARD®

Visit Hal Leonard Online at
www.halleonard.com

Contact Us:
Hal Leonard
7777 West Bluemound Road
Milwaukee, WI 53213
Email: info@halleonard.com

In Europe contact:
Hal Leonard Europe Limited
Distribution Centre, Newmarket Road
Bury St Edmunds, Suffolk, IP33 3YB
Email: info@halleonardeurope.com

In Australia contact:
Hal Leonard Australia Pty. Ltd.
4 Lentara Court
Cheltenham, Victoria, 3192 Australia
Email: info@halleonard.com.au

INTRODUCTION

"It is always darkest just before the day dawneth" wrote Thomas Fuller in 1650, perhaps committing to paper some folk wisdom of the time. This uplifting thought, that even in the darkest moments one can let in the light of hope, was at the forefront of Churchill's thoughts when in May 1940 he took on the task to convince the British people to fight what might have already looked like a lost war. His irrepressible energy, but also his many doubts, are the engines that powered him through those treacherous months at the beginning of the war. The music for Darkest Hour is, in many ways, the voice of Churchill's restlessness, his pacing up and down the war rooms, looking for the dawn that he himself, eventually, helped to make possible.

Dario Marianelli

PRELUDE

by Dario Marianelli

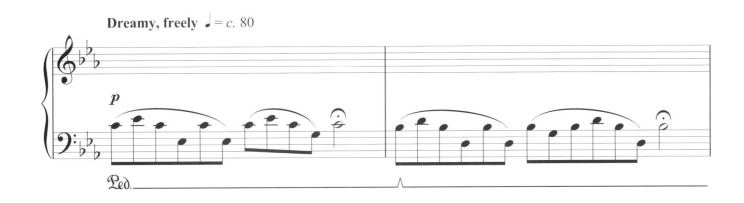

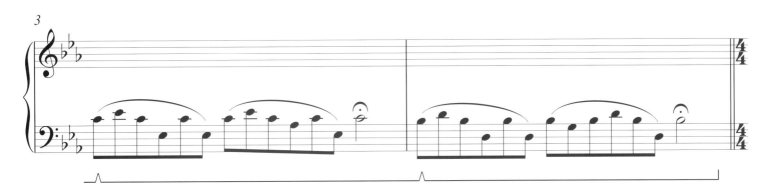

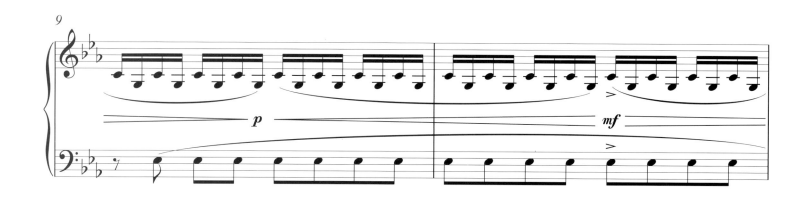

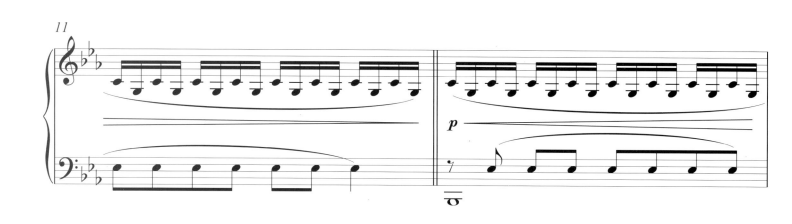

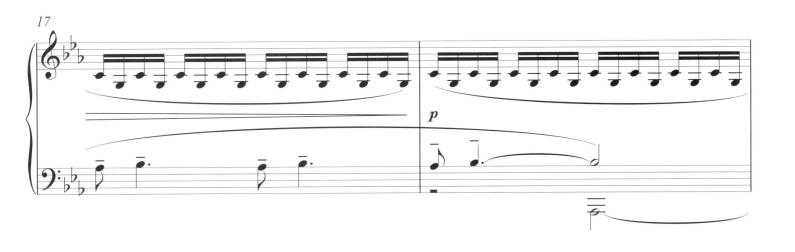

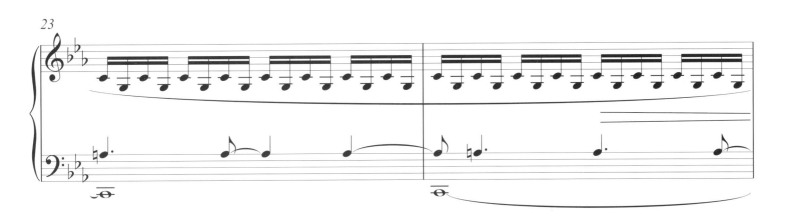

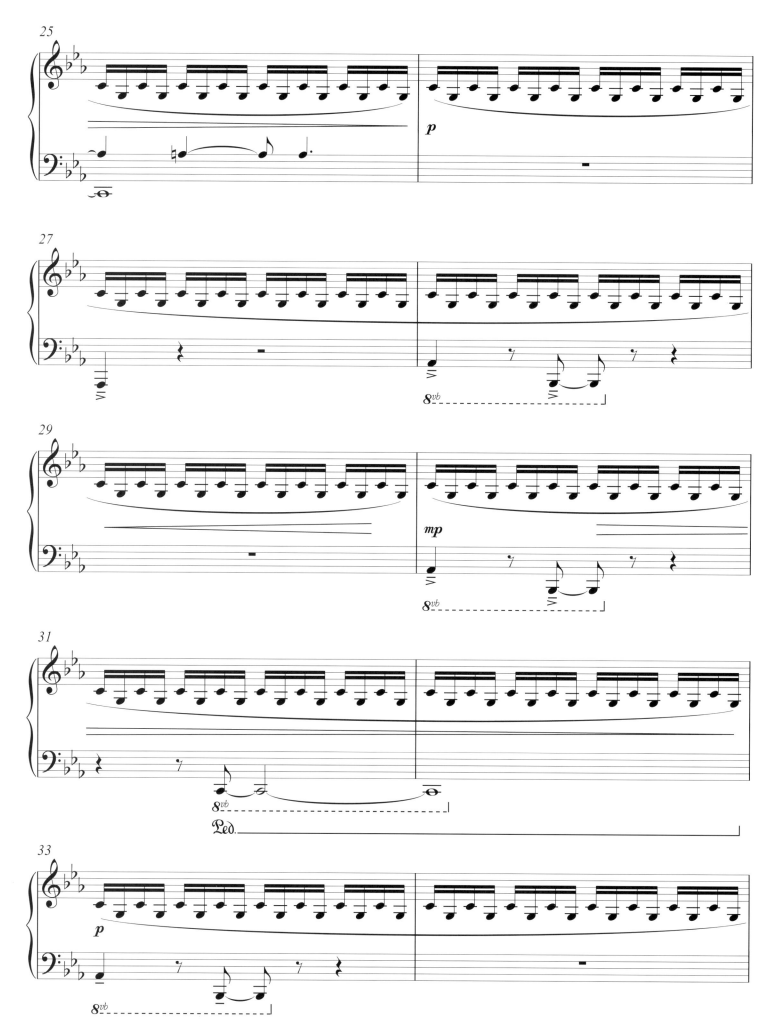

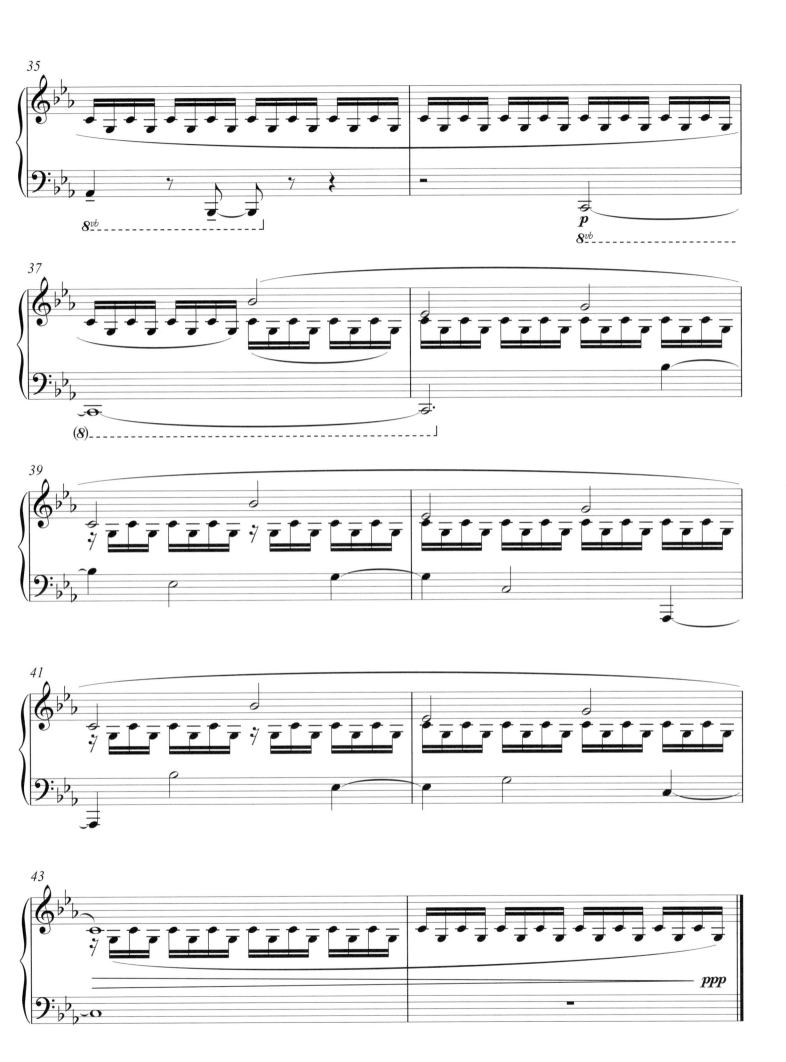

A TELEGRAM FROM THE PALACE

by Dario Marianelli

11

WINSTON AND GEORGE

by Dario Marianelli

ONE OF THEM

by Dario Marianelli

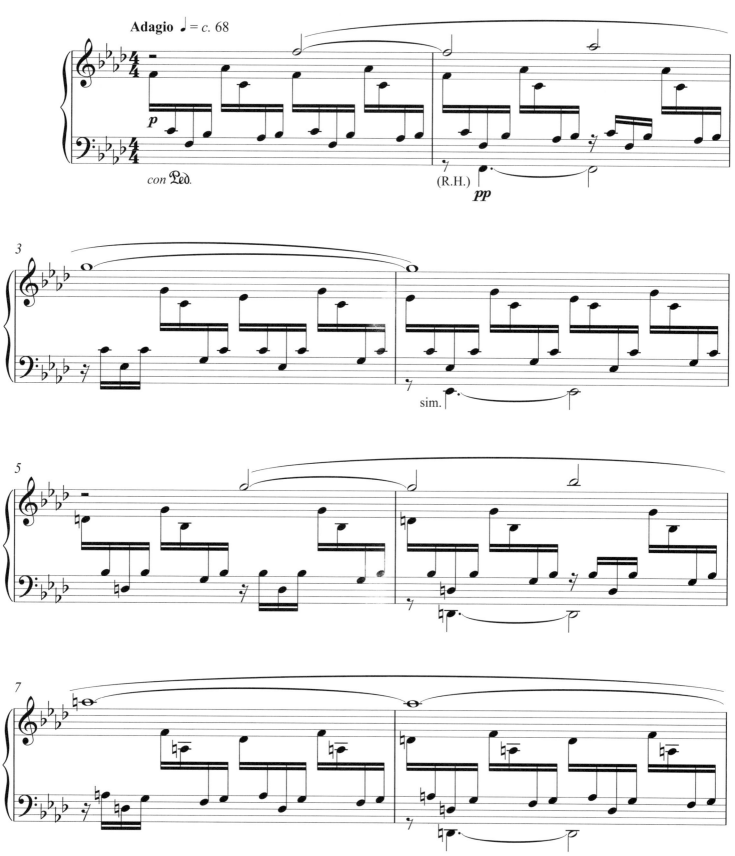

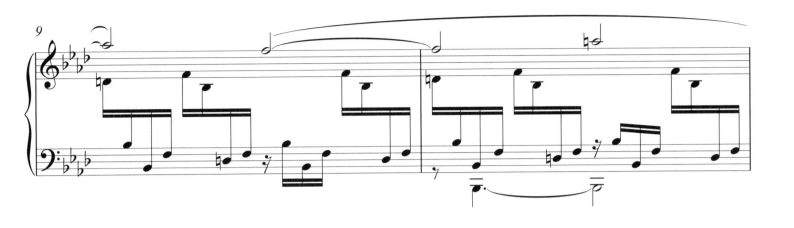

FIRST SPEECH TO THE COMMONS

by Dario Marianelli

(sempre leggero e stacc.)

L.H.

(R.H.)

THE WAR ROOMS

by Dario Marianelli

FROM THE AIR

by Dario Marianelli

RADIO BROADCAST

by Dario Marianelli

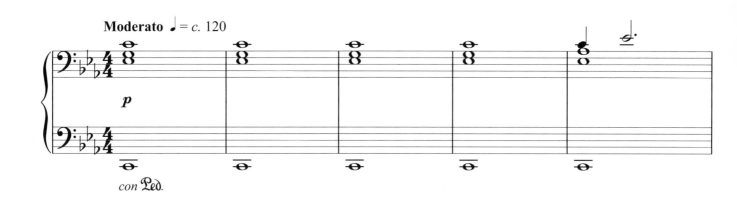

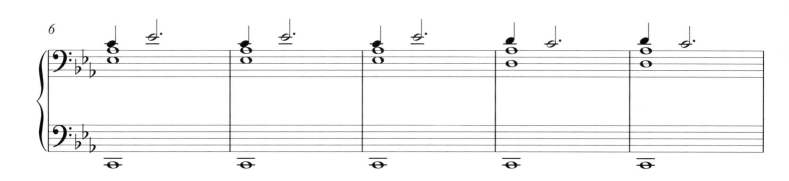

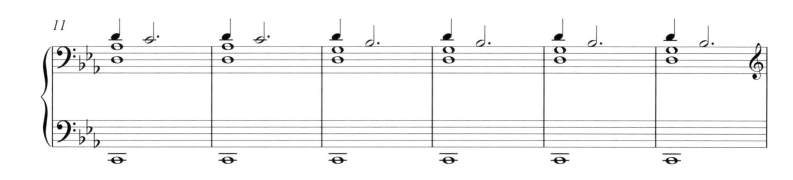

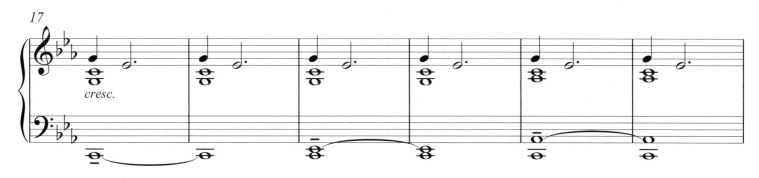

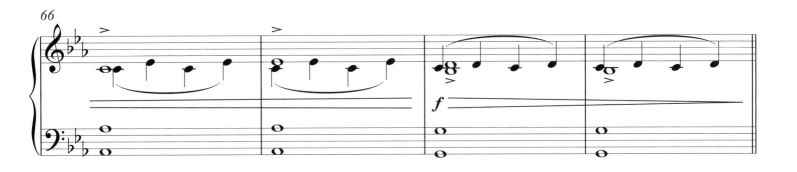

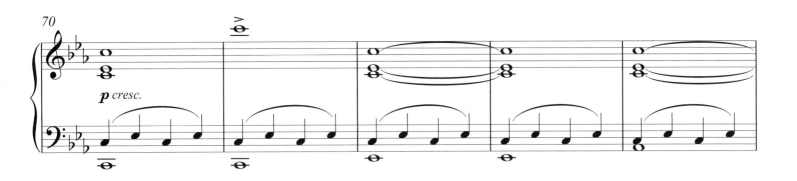

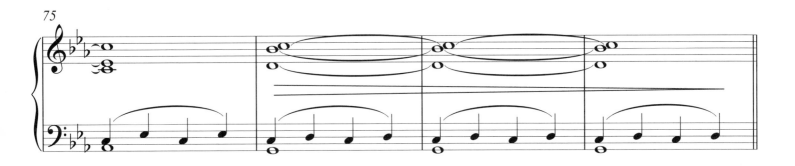

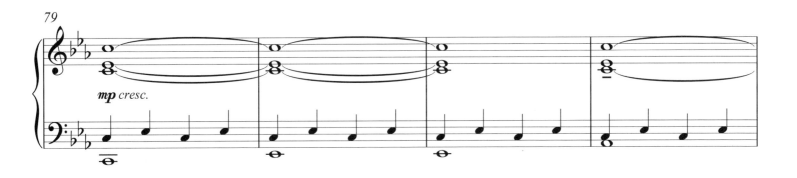

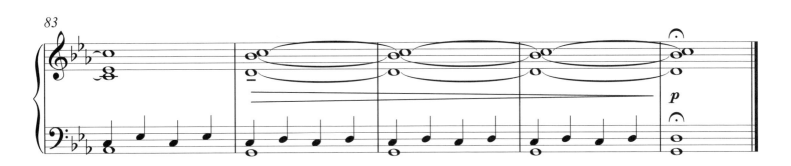

I WOULDN'T TRUST HIM WITH MY BICYCLE

by Dario Marianelli

AN ULTIMATUM

by Dario Marianelli

THE WORDS WON'T COME

by Dario Marianelli

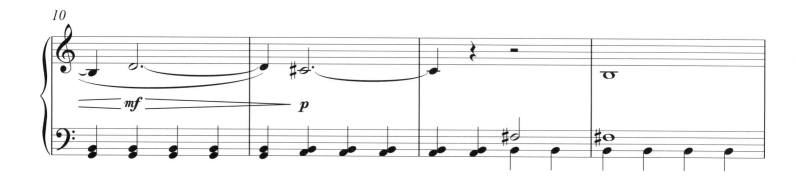

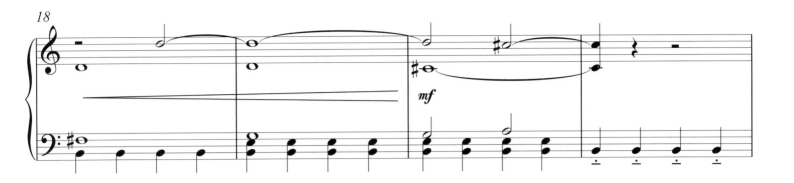

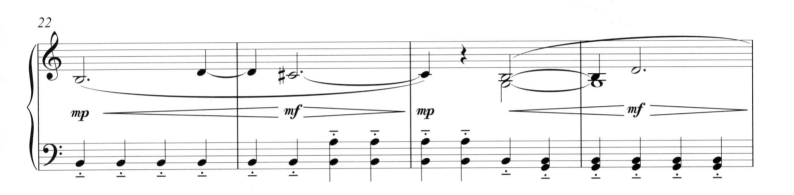

DISTRICT LINE, EAST, ONE STOP.

by Dario Marianelli

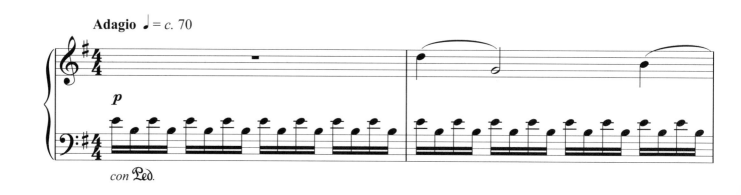

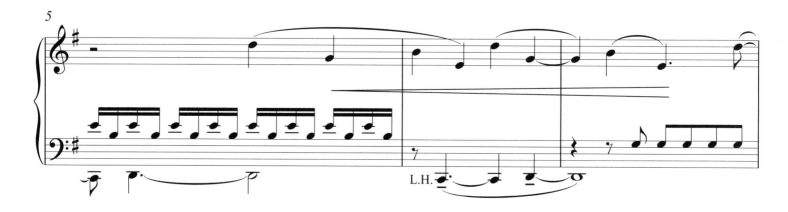

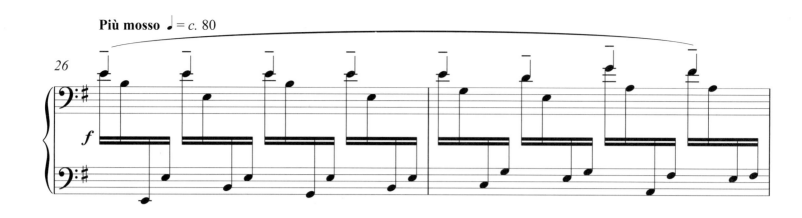

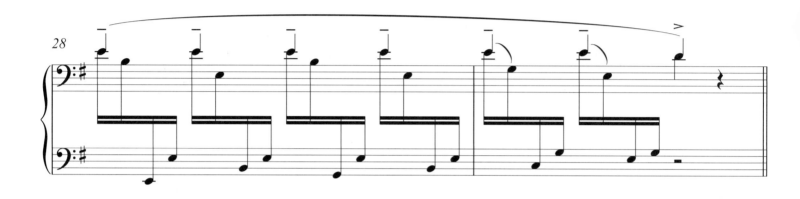

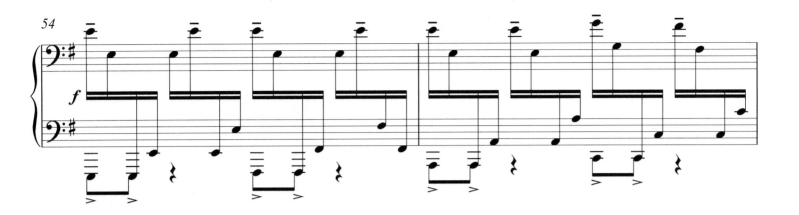

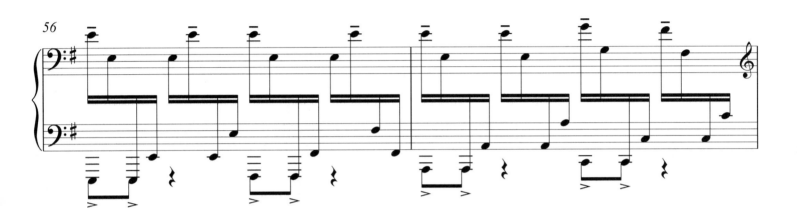

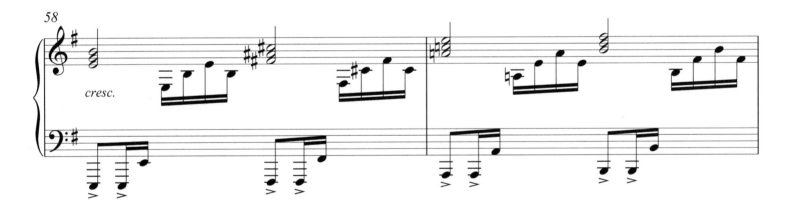

WE SHALL FIGHT

by Dario Marianelli

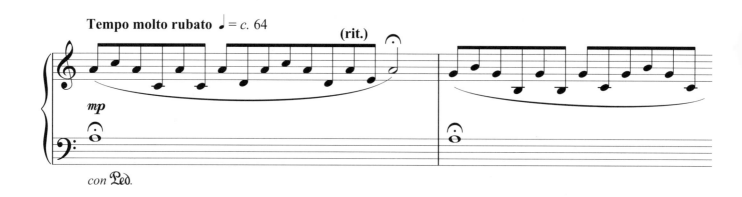

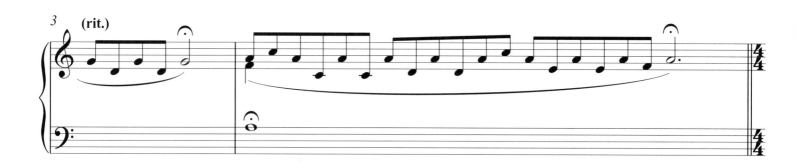

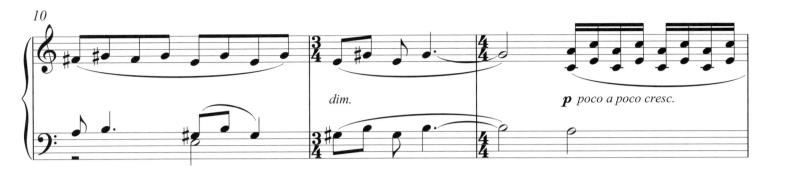

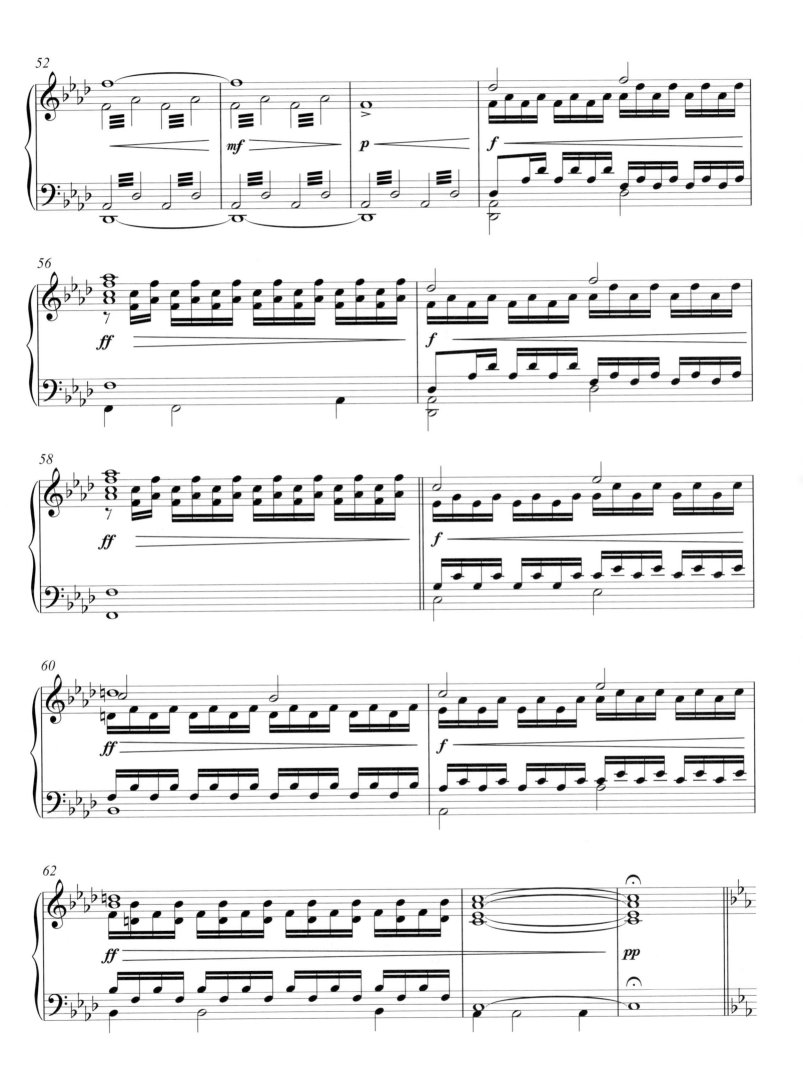

for Víkingur Ólaffson

DARKEST HOUR

by Dario Marianelli

Allegro ♩ = c. 112

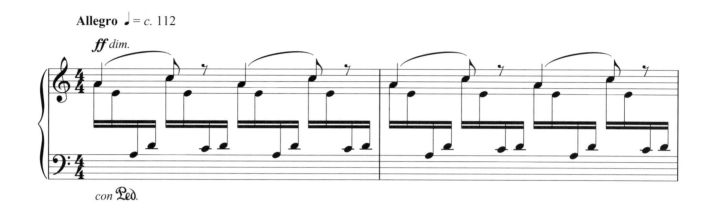

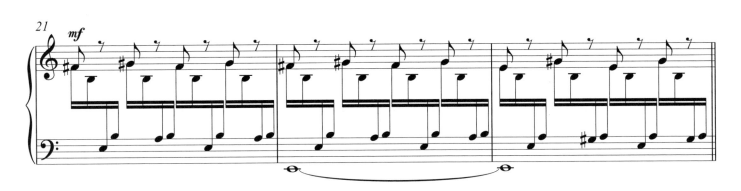

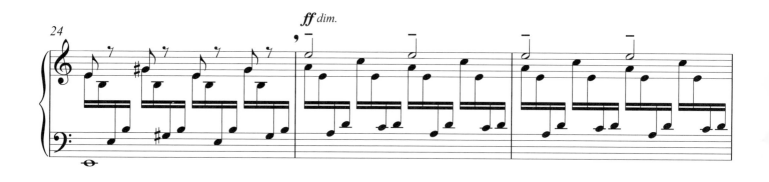

WE MUST PREPARE
FOR IMMINENT INVASION

by Dario Marianelli

Moderato ♩ = c. 114

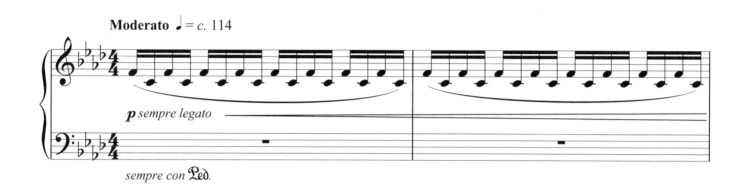

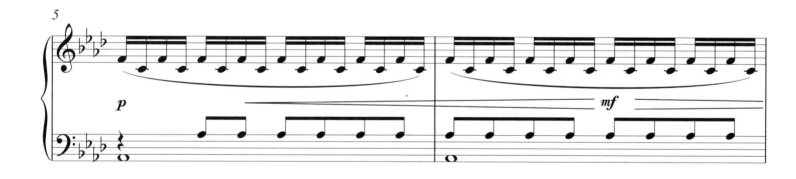

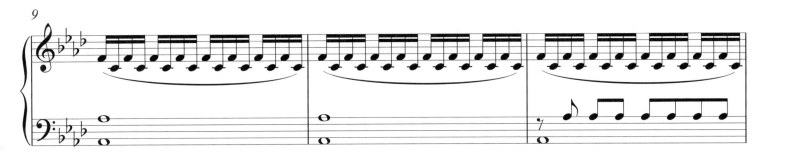

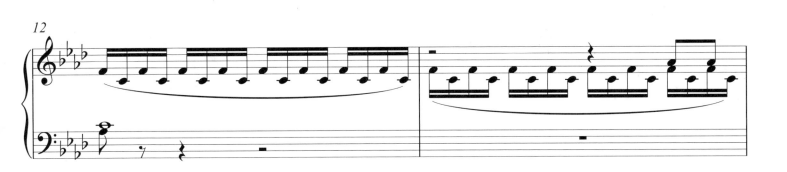

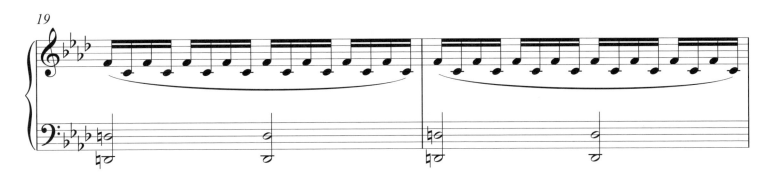

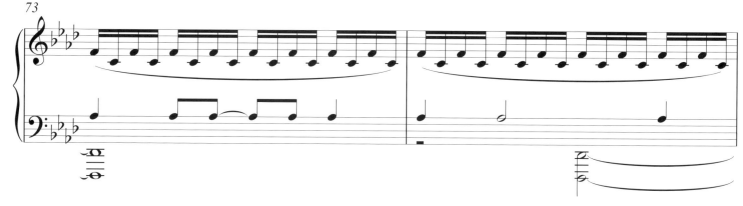

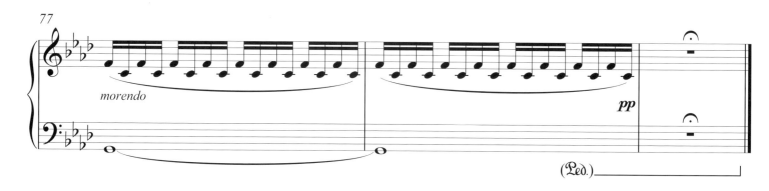

ORIGINAL MUSIC BY DARIO MARIANELLI.
EDITED BY JAMES WELLAND.
ADDITIONAL ARRANGEMENTS BY ALISTAIR WATSON.
MUSIC PROCESSED BY SARAH LOFTHOUSE, SEL MUSIC ART LTD.
ADDITIONAL DESIGN BY TIM FIELD.
PRINTED IN THE EU.

VISIT HAL LEONARD ONLINE AT
WWW.HALLEONARD.COM

FOCUS FEATURES PRESENTS IN ASSOCIATION WITH PERFECT WORLD PICTURES A WORKING TITLE PRODUCTION A JOE WRIGHT FILM GARY OLDMAN "DARKEST HOUR"
KRISTIN SCOTT THOMAS LILY JAMES STEPHEN DILLANE AND BEN MENDELSOHN CASTING BY JINA JAY MUSIC BY DARIO MARIANELLI COSTUME DESIGNER JACQUELINE DURRAN
EDITOR VALERIO BONELLI PRODUCTION DESIGNER SARAH GREENWOOD DIRECTOR OF PHOTOGRAPHY BRUNO DELBONNEL AFC ASC EXECUTIVE PRODUCERS JAMES BIDDLE LUCAS WEBB LIZA CHASIN WRITTEN BY ANTHONY McCARTEN
PRODUCED BY TIM BEVAN ERIC FELLNER LISA BRUCE ANTHONY McCARTEN DOUGLAS URBANSKI DIRECTED BY JOE WRIGHT